Lessons for the Heart:
52 Ways to Share God with Children
Volume 2

Cheryle Renee-Chapman Hanna

Cheryle Hanna Ministries
Detroit, Michigan

Lessons for the Heart
Copyright © 2019 Cheryle Renee-Chapman Hanna

Book cover design by Edge Designs

Music Transcription by Myk'l Hanna

Printed in the United States of America

Web Address: lessons4theheart.com

ISBN: 978-0-578-22037-6

For my youngest heart, Myles

Yaya

Foreword

I love that moment in the worship service when little children walk down the aisle and find a place where they can stand or sit and hear a gospel message tailored just for them. To hear adults, break down the gospel into bite-sized bits of knowledge for their special audience is a congregation's sacred witness that children are special, welcomed, and worthy of our time and attention in the faith. Many congregations believe, as I do, that Christian nurture begins with attentiveness and compassion for our youngest members. That no matter the age, all are able to comprehend lessons from the Bible and develop a spiritual vocabulary of love, grace, mercy, joy, contentment, self-sacrifice, and other spiritual values.

Children's sermons are important because they help to train children to listen to biblical stories in a different way: rather than have children sitting together in a classroom to draw biblical figures or read Bible verses, children are placed in a special spotlight and have to pay careful attention to what is spoken.

Over time, they acquire the ability to listen, learn, and develop their own beliefs about the truth of God's word. Children learn lessons on telling the truth, helping others, Jesus Christ feeding the multitudes, and dying on the Cross for our sins. As important, these messages help nurture children's sensitivity to injustices and how to become those who aspire to be young agents to help the world to be fairer and more just.

To deny children the opportunity to hear a sermon tailored for them deprives them of the ability to stand on their own and begin to articulate their faith. Dr. Hanna writes, children have the ability to grow because they are "God's seeds," able to "grow in wisdom and strength and do amazing things in God's kingdom." To do amazing things, children should be assisted with as many instruments of instruction as possible; the children's sermon is a powerful instrument of instruction and growth.

Dr. Hanna has dedicated a major focus of her ministry to children's Christian nurture. Hundreds of children have benefitted from her sermons and guidance over the years because she has a generous spirit for children. In this second volume of sermons, she has expressed this generosity through diverse biblical sermon themes such as living in peace and harmony, learning to trust in God, and God's love for us through Jesus's sacrifice on the Cross. In the end, Dr. Hanna's greatest prayer for children is one we all share: "Help our children to give of themselves and heal and help the world. Amen."

Pamela James Jones, Ph.D.

Historian of Christianity

Adjunct Faculty, Philosophy and Religion

Central Michigan University

Mt. Pleasant, Michigan

Introduction

Deuteronomy 31:12-13

Assemble the people—men, women and children, and the foreigners residing in your towns—so they can listen and learn to fear the LORD your God and follow carefully all the words of this law.
Their children, who do not know this law, must hear it and learn to fear the LORD your God as long as you live in the land you are crossing the Jordan to possess."

I gave my first Lesson for the Heart in 1999. On each successive Sunday, I gave the message I would give planning and thought but never had a written script. In 2016, a local pastor had to be away from his family for several months and I began sharing the morning lessons with the pastor's young sons. My intention was to check in on them and encourage them. After the pastor returned, I thought I would be relieved of my sharing, but the boys looked forward to the weekly lessons. I began writing down the lessons so others could share them in my absence and *Lessons for the Heart* was born.

Lessons for the Heart, Volume 2 is my continued intention to encourage those two young people and the many children, youth and adults listening for God's word in a way which comforts, challenges and strengthens. The 52 new lessons pick up where Volume 1 ended and contain more singing, moving, laughing than the first.

There is a Sunday is every week and if you have been assigned or designated to speak to the children, don't be scared. *Lessons for the Heart, Volume 2* is biblically aligned and theologically responsible with a lesson, props and a prayer needed for a wonderful time with the children. Whether you are a Solo Pastor who could use a little help every now and then, an Associate Pastor called o pitch in at the last minute or a parent or grandparent excited about sharing your faith; *Lessons for the Heart, Volume 2* will instill confidence and skill as you share God with the children in your life.

The *Lessons for the Heart, Volume 2* includes, purchasing suggestions, music and instructions to make buttons, pins, and cards. The goal is reaching the hearts of children with God.

I pray a blessing on you and on your children as your connection with God grows stronger and sweeter each day.

Cheryle Hanna

1   Table Talk   Luke 14:1, 7-14

Supplies: Pieces of cotton cloth or paper 17" square, (it is okay if slightly smaller or larger) small treats to place inside folded napkins. https://foodal.com/knowledge/how-to/napkin-folding/

A lesson for the heart

Dinner time is a great opportunity for families to catch up. At the table, we are free to ask questions, tell jokes and stories while surrounded by people who love and care about us. Sometimes the dinner is more like a banquet where extended family and friends are included. These are grand occasions with lots of food and special decorations. When the special napkins appear, it is a good sign a special dinner is coming.

Daily God sets a grand table before us. We have clear water to drink, homes with electricity and comfortable beds to sleep. God is good. We are free to ask God questions, tell jokes and a story with the guarantee God loves us.

To remind you of God's special table, I have a napkin for you. It is folded and like the love of God, there is something sweet inside—just because.

Let us Pray: God of abundance and love, thank you for the table of blessings we enjoy. Help our children always come to you and share their lives, feelings and thoughts knowing you love them. Bless our children with your continued abundance and give them generous hearts to share what they receive. Amen

1st Sunday September

2   Brewster Millions   Luke 14:25-33

Supplies: Bags of treats!

A lesson for the heart

Imagine you are given a gift of 30 million dollars—the gift comes with one catch; you must give away all the money within the 30 days. This is the plot of the 1985 movie starring Richard Pryor entitled "Brewster's Millions."

[spoiler alert—it was very hard, but Brewster did it!]

We live in a very similar movie every day of our lives. God gives us millions of gifts in the form of talent, intellect, and opportunities and we are called by God to share those gifts with the world. When we share the world is better and we are richer.

This bag of treats is an example of your 'millions'. Please share and be blessed.

Let us pray: Thank you God for the many 'millions' you give. Bless our children to be generous and kind, sharing your gifts with others. Amen

2nd Sunday September

3   Hide and Seek   Luke 15:1-10

Supplies: Toy or candy sheep

A lesson for the heart

In the game of 'Hide and Seek,' one person attempts to find all the others hiding nearby. Sometimes if we pick a good hiding place it can take a while for the person to find us, but we don't worry, we know someone is looking for us.

God is the best at 'hide and seek', no matter where you go or how lost feel; God is always looking for you and when you are reunited with God, heaven celebrates.

God is the good shepherd and you are God's little sheep and God is always looking for and after you.

God will always find you.

Take these sheep as symbols of your place in God's kingdom.

Let us pray: Merciful God, when our children are lost please never tire in your search; bringing them safely home. Amen

3rd Sunday September

4   Choose Wisely   Luke 16:1-3

Supplies: Chocolate and Caramel candy

A lesson for the heart

Every day we make dozens of choices.
Do I wear green or blue pants?
Do I let my hair down or do I wear a hat?
Frosted Flakes of Coco Puffs for breakfast?
Do I speak up while my classmate is teased or made fun of?

Many of our choices have no consequences, other choices can last a lifetime. God has placed teachers, family and church members in your lives to help you make good choices. Your teachers share the best possible methods and decision-making skills. Your family shows you right from wrong and corrects misbehavior. Best of all they share the word of God with you. When we read and learn scripture, we make the best choices of all.

God chose you. God wants you to grow strong, smart and spirit filled.

One last choice--do you want chocolate or caramel?

Let us pray: Holy God, of the many choices, we are glad you chose us. Please guide our children to choose you. Amen

4th Sunday September

5   Live Generously   2 Corinthians 8:7-9

Supplies: 'Coins' enough to share generously. (Candy coins work very well.)

A lesson for the heart

Generosity is a virtue and a practice. When we are generous, our actions speak loudly. Generosity makes the world a better place by repairing what is broken around us.

God gave us Jesus as an example and a pattern of generosity. Jesus was always ready to heal and help everyone. And later the church at Corinth was promised they would never lack if they gave generously.

I am giving you a handful of coins. Consider something you could do with theses 'coins' to heal and help someone. God loves a cheerful giver.

Let us pray: Generous and gracious God. Thank you for giving us enough to share. Help our children to give of themselves and heal and help the world. Amen

5th Sunday September

6　　Small Seeds

Supplies: packages of popcorn

A lesson for the heart

This is harvest season. Farmers are collecting the fruit and vegetables from their orchards and fields. It may be difficult to imagine that every stalk of grain and every ripened fruit started and grew from a seed.

(Show them some corn seeds)

From these small seeds will grow many, many ears of corn.

You are God's seeds. Like the kernels of corn, you were created by God to grow and multiply. You may be small now, but you will grow in wisdom and strength and do amazing things in God's kingdom.

Another good thing about corn seeds, when they are roasted, they make POPCORN.

Let us pray: Holy God, thank you for making our children your seed. Help them grow straight and multiply. Amen

1st Sunday October

7   Soapy Clean   Luke 17:11-19

Supplies: Small bars of soap

A lesson for the heart

It can be fun to play outside in the dirt, make mud pies, and create tunnels or moats. With enough dirt, imagination is the only limit and almost anything is possible.

When the fun is over someone will want us to wash off the dirt. They will give us soap and we will use the soap to make us clean.

Like the soap we use to remove the dirt and stains after playing outside, God's grace, mercy and forgiveness cleanses us completely no matter how dirty our lives or our ways.

This soap will make you clean on the outside and your faith in God will keep you clean on the inside.

Let us pray: Merciful God, we love you and thank you for your grace, mercy and forgiveness making us clean. Keep our children clean, inside and out! Amen

2nd Sunday October

8 God is Fair

Luke 18:1-8

Supplies: Chocolate candy bars.

A lesson for the heart

Imagine with me someone offering to share a candy bar with you. They break the candy into two pieces, but the pieces are not equal. In order to make the two pieces even they take a large bite out of the larger piece and then announces, "Now they are even" as they hand you the second piece. Few would think the person sharing the candy was being fair.

God is not a friend offering to split a candy bar. God treats everyone fairly. God loves everyone and shares equally the gifts of the world with everyone who asks.

God is fair.

You don't need to share this candy bar with anyone, it is all yours.

Let us pray: Thank you God for being God. There is none like you. We are happy you are God and treat us fairly. Please hear the prayers of our children, today and always. Amen

3rd Sunday October

9 Prayerful Hands   Luke 18:9-14

Supplies: Cookies in the shape of hands. Hand Shaped cookie cutters available in Canada at Bulk Barn and online from Amazon. The cheap and dirty method is prepacked sugar cookie dough; the adventurous could mix up a batch of homemade! (Don't forget the sprinkles)

A lesson for the heart

Prayer is a conversation with God.
We can use our hands to help us pray.

(Thumb) God, thank you for Jesus Christ.

(Pointer finger) God, thank you for my mom, dad, and siblings.

(Middle finger) God, take care of my pastor, elected and appointed officials.

(Ring finger) God, protect persons serving God and the church in far away and remote places.

(Baby finger) Please God, take care of the little people, unseen but important to us, like the postal carrier, grocer and bus drivers.

Gracious God, thank you for all you have done, are doing and will do in the lives of our children. Give them all hearts filled with gratitude and praise. Amen

4th Sunday October

Supplies: Learn the sung below. It is an old camp song, largely modified. Print the song as an invitation from God. for the children.

A lesson for the heart

Verse 1
The other day (echo)
I met Je-sus, (echo)
I didn't want to make a fuss.
(echo from the beginning)

Verse 2
God said to me, (echo)
Why don't you come? (echo)
Come on with me and have some fun.
(echo from the beginning)

Verse 3
And so, I went (echo)
With God that day. (echo)
I've learned to love, to share and pray.
(echo from the beginning)

Remember, no matter who you are or what you are doing, God wants to be in your company.

Let us pray: Thank you God for inviting us to join you. Help us to extend the invitation to others. Amen

1st Sunday November

The Other Day

Lessons for the Heart Vol. 2

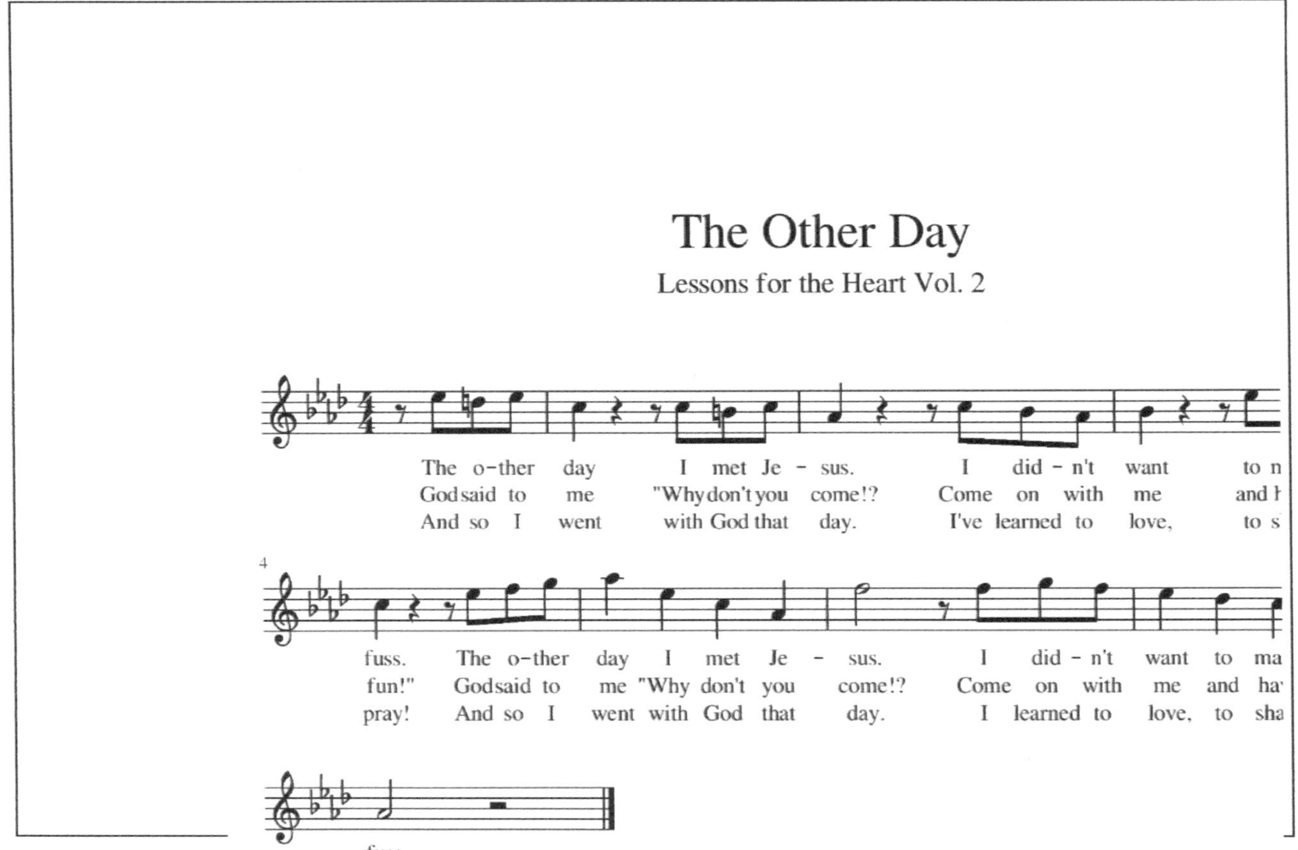

11   Resurrection Cookies   Luke 20:27-38

Supplies: Bake the Resurrection Cookies

A lesson for the heart

Today let's talk about a big church word -- Resurrection. Resurrection means coming back from death. As followers of Jesus Christ, we do not believe Jesus is dead, we believe Jesus rose from the grave and lives.
Because Jesus lives, we also have a life with Jesus, forever.

These cookies will help me explain. Last night I placed these cookies in the oven. I closed the oven door and left them inside. This morning when I opened the oven, the cookies were empty.

This is what we believe about Jesus. Jesus was left in the tomb on Friday night but on Sunday morning the tomb was empty.
The cookies are also very tasty. Take one or two!

Let us pray: All powerful Saviour, we are grateful the tomb was empty, and that Jesus lives. Bless our children to know Christ and God's resurrection power, today and always. Amen

2nd Sunday November

Resurrection Cookies

1 tsp. vinegar
3 egg whites
1 c. sugar
1 pinch of salt
1 c. chopped pecans

On the Saturday before Easter, preheat the oven to 300 degrees.

To a medium bowl add vinegar, the egg whites, a pinch of salt, and sugar. Beat 11-15 minutes until stiff peaks form. Fold in the chopped nuts. Drop a teaspoon at a time onto waxed paper-covered baking sheet. Put the baking sheet into the oven and turn the oven OFF.
Go to bed.

On Resurrection Morning, open the oven. The cookies will have a cracked surface and be empty inside.

Christ has Risen!
Christ has Risen Indeed!

12   Jenga   Luke 21:5-19

Supplies: building block candy and a Jenga game to display.

A lesson for the Heart

'Jenga' is a game[1]. At the start all the pieces are stacked into a tower. The players take turns removing one of the pieces and placing the piece on top of the tower. The tower gets taller and less stable. Soon the tower falls.

Sometimes it seems humanity is playing 'Jenga' building towers which will fall rather than building people. God is more interested in the lives of people than the brick and mortar of buildings.

These bags are filled with candy building blocks. They will not last and that is the point. Only the good we do for Christ will last. Share the candy and enjoy building lives and love with people. God's kingdom will be taller for it.

Let us pray: Gracious Saviour, thank you for caring more about us than buildings. Please bless our children to love in the same way. Amen

3rd Sunday November

---

[1] Jenga was created by Leslie Scott and currently is marketed by Hasbro.

13   King Jesus   Luke 23:33-43

A lesson for the heart

This weekend worshipping communities world-wide celebrate Christ-the-King Sunday and Sabbath. We honor Jesus Christ as the one who reigns in the kingdom of God.

Kings and Queens care about the people of the kingdom.

Kings and Queens share what they must to help others.

Most importantly, Kings and Queens make sacrifices for the kingdom.

Jesus Christ is our reigning king and Jesus wants you to continue the work of God and share in kingdom building. God's calling makes you royalty—you are like kings and queens.

Wear these crowns to display your willingness to build God's kingdom and people.

Let us pray: Holy God, bless our children to be gracious and kind and generous builders of your kingdom. Amen

4th Sunday November

14   War and Peace   Isaiah 2:1-5

Supplies: Equal number of empty shot gun shells, (try the local gun range) birthday candles and Dove brand candy.

A lesson for the heart

We want peace, but if we watch TV or listen to our parents talk—we know war and disagreements are everywhere.

Our job is to take the things of war and give them new purpose. This can be difficult. I have something which should help. The first thing is an empty shot gun shell. All the shot and powder, which can hurt people, has been removed. The second thing is a purple candle. The candle is a symbol of the hope we have in God.

When we place the candle in the empty shell, the shell becomes a candle holder. We changed a thing of war into a tool of peace and when the candle is lit it casts out the darkest and shines the light of God.

The final thing is Dove candy—the dove is the symbol of peace, when you eat the candy think of the peace of God and peace of God's coming into the world.

Let us pray: Holy God, thank you for your peace. Cover our children and make them strong and creative so they may turn the things of war into the tools of peace. Amen

Advent 1

Supplies: Animal Crackers/Cookies

A lesson for the heart

Please take these packages of animal crackers and carefully examine the animals inside. Notice the creatures in the box of Animal Crackers don't fight.
The camels don't spit.
The Lions don't hunt, and the snakes don't bite. All the animals live together in complete peace.

I think God is pleased with the example set by the animal crackers and would love for all creatures to live in harmony and peace.

We can pretend we live in a box of animal crackers. We can practice not growling at persons who upset us. We can practice not biting people who make us angry and we can be polite and civil to everyone we meet.
We can try. God will help.

Let us pray: Merciful God and Prince of Peace. Help us to live together in peace. Bless our children to be the peace the world needs and bless the world to show our children peace in return. Amen

Advent 2

Supplies: stickers of flowers. (Jolee's Boutique Dimensional Stickers, Dogwood and Crocus available on Amazon)

A lesson for the heart

Persons living in the northern half of the globe do not expect to see fields of blooming flowers this time of the year. Flowers require the warmth of the sun and water to grow. It would be lovely; few sights can bring as much joy.

Long ago God promised to come into the world and be present with humanity. God sent Jesus to bring God's joy. In Jesus' presence we see, smell, and hear a world filled with love, peace, joy and acceptance of all people.

Being in the presence of God is like being surrounded by blooming flowers. God has come and wants to give you that joy, peace, love and acceptance. Only believe.

Let us prayer: Blessed Saviour, thank you for coming into the world and making it like a field of blooming flowers. We want to welcome you today and every day and to experience your joy, always. Amen

Advent 3

17   Immanuel   Isaiah 7:10-16

Supplies: Heart shaped cookies or candy. Learn the chorus of John Lennon's song, "All you Need is Love"[2]

A lesson for the heart

The late John Lennon and the Beatles had a great song, that went something like this:

(singing) *All you need is love.*

All you need is love, love

Love is all you need.

John Lennon may not have been singing about God but since God is love I think God would approve. God loved the world so much, God sent Jesus. Jesus talked, prayed and preached love.

(singing) *All you need is love, love. Love is all you need.*

 Love and heart shaped goodies!

Let us pray: God, who is love, thank you for sending your so Jesus to us. Thank you for the message of love Christ brings. May love live in the hearts of your children always. Amen

Advent 4

---

[2] Songwriter John Lennon, Paul McCartney; Sony/ATV Music Publishing LLC

18   Angel Food   Matthew 2:13-23

Supplies: Angel Cake. YouTube the Nolan Williams song, "Angels Watching over Me"

A lesson for the heart

The writer of the gospel of Matthew tells the story of angels coming to Jesus' father, Joseph. In the first dream an angel tells joseph of Jesus' birth and in the second dream an angel warns Joseph to take the young family to Egypt for a time before returning to the land of Israel.

Angels are God's messengers and to this day bring words of protection and guidance. Sometimes God's angel may look like everyone else – so keep your hearts open and always ready to hear from God.

I think a song may help you remember. The song was written in 1969 by Nolan Williams. It goes something like this,

"All night, all day angels watching over me my Lord! All night, all day angels watching over me!"

Let us pray: Holy God, please send your angles to watch over our children, giving them guidance and protection all the days of their lives. Amen

5th Sunday December

19   Identity/It's in You   John 1: [1-9] 10-18

Supplies: An almost empty tube of toothpaste and travel sized tubes of tooth paste to share.

A lesson for the heart

The makers of your favorite toothpaste begin with an empty tube. A seal and cap are placed on one end and toothpaste is pushed in the back end; then the end is crimped and sealed. When you squeeze, you never worry that something other than toothpaste will come out. Never! You trust the makers of the toothpaste. Sometimes it may take a bit of effort but what comes out is toothpaste.

When God made you, everything you need to be the person God intended was placed inside. Sometimes things come easy and other times it may take a bit more effort—don't dismay—it's in you! God, like the manufacturer of the toothpaste has filled you with good stuff all the way to the end. It's in you!

When things are a little bit difficult or take a little more work—pull out your tube, squeeze it, taste a little to remind yourself its still toothpaste.

Let us pray: Gracious and compassionate God, thank you for making us so well. Help our children to trust you when life is easy and when life takes a bit more effort. Amen

1st Sunday January

Supplies: Candy bones

A lesson for the heart

(start in chanting)

The foot bone is connected to the leg-bone.

The leg bone is connected to the knee-bone.

The knee-bone is connected to the thigh bone.

The thigh bone connected to the backbone.

The backbone connected to the neck bone.

Now hear the word of the Lord.

God knows you inside and outside. You were born with intention, purpose and love from God. The love from God, given to you before you were born can never be lost or denied. God loves you inside and outside and there is nothing you can do about it!

These bones are a lot like the ones inside your body—only eatable and sweeter---eat up!

Let us pray: Thank you God for knowing the children inside and out. Please bless them to continue to grow in statue and in grace. Amen

3rd Sunday January

21   Simon Says   Matthew 4:12-23

Supplies: Name badges which read: Follow Me

A lesson for the heart

A great game to play inside or out is 'Simon Says'. One person is Simon and everyone else must do what Simon says. For example, Simon says 'clap your hands'. Simon says, 'stump your feet.' 'touch your head.' If you touched your head, you are eliminated because Simon didn't say it!

God is the ultimate 'Simon' giving us daily instructions through the words written within the scripture. When we read our bibles and pray, God shares the way to live, grow and be all we were created to be. When we follow God, others will follow us, and the kingdom will grow and grow!

Wear this badge. It will let the world know you follow God and the world will follow you!

Let us pray: Almighty God, thank for great leadership. Help our children to follow you always and let others follow them to you. Amen

4th Sunday January

Supplies: Chocolate Chip Cookies

A lesson for the heart

Once upon a time there lived nine happy children.

The nine didn't have much money – and they were happy. They didn't have the largest television on the block or the large premium cable package, and they were happy. They didn't have the newest version of "Just Dance[3]" on their home computer, and they were happy.

The nine were happy because they knew God loved and cared for them.

You can be just as happy. Remember you are made in the image and likeness of God and God loves you to the moon and back.

I love you too that is why I brought chocolate chip cookies. Let's be happy together!

Let us pray: Oh God, bless are children to know your love for them, today, tomorrow and always. Amen

1st Sunday February

---

[3]Just Dance 2019 is a video game by Ubisoft

23   Salty

Matthew 5: 13-20

Supplies: Saltwater Taffy

A lesson for the heart

Salt is a good thing. Think of pretzels, popcorn or salted caramel ice cream. Salt is also good for cleaning and preserving. The best cooks would never think of preparing a chicken without salt.

Salt is a good thing. Yet, if salt stops being salty it is only good for throwing on the ground.

God wants us to be salty. When we pray and read God's word it keeps us salty. Our connection with God cleans any meanness from our hearts and preserve the life and dignity of our community. Salt is a good thing.

Another good thing about salt is Saltwater Taffy—let's get salty!

Let us pray: God who cleans and preserves, please remove any uncleanliness from the hearts of our children and keep them whole and well preserved their life long. Amen

2nd Sunday February

Matthew 5:1-37

Supplies: Rolls of 'Duct Tape"[4]

A lesson for the heart

Long ago someone wrote,

"Sticks and Stones may break your bones, but words can never hurt you."

I am sure the author meant well but words can and do hurt. Words can break our heart, tear our spirit and destroy our confidence.

God would never hurt you and God would never want us to hurt anyone with sticks, stones or words. On the rare occasion we find we have hurt someone; we are to go quickly and patch things up.

Duct tape is used the world over to patch broken, torn and damaged things. Keep this duct tape nearby to remind you to always be ready to patch things with family, friends and even enemies.

Let us pray: Merciful God, thank you for patching things up for us. Encourage our children never to hurt anyone and always be ready to patch things up. Amen

3rd Sunday February

---

[4] www.tapeplanet.com for rolls on sale under $1.00/roll.

Supplies: Pikachu toys or candy[5]

A lesson for the heart

Pikachu[6] may be the cutest and most adorable Pokémon of all times, kind, cuddly and considerate. But don't like the soft exterior fool you, when Pikachu is exposed to a Thunderstorm, she transfigures into Raichu, a much more powerful version of herself.

God has a transformation planned for you. God wants you to experience the 'Thunderstorm of Holy Presence' and become a more powerful version of yourself.

With the holy power of God, you will change the world. You will see injustice on the playground and speak out. You will hear your classmates are hungry and share your lunch. You will be transfigured.

Let us pray: Sweet Holy Spirit, enter the hearts of our children, transfigure them to be more like Jesus, growing more loving each day of their lives. Amen

4th Sunday February

---

[5] https://www.etsy.com/ca/listing/554039564/12-x-pikachu-pokemon-stand-up-edible
[6] Pikachu is a character of Pokémon a media franchise managed by the Pokémon Company, a Japanese consortium between Nintendo, Game Freak and Creatures.

26   Slow Down   Matthew 4:1-11

Supplies: Small Stones

A lesson for the heart

For the next forty days the church celebrates Jesus' days in the wilderness. We call this time Lent.

The word 'lent' in French is translated into English as 'slow'. It is a caution to reduce our speed when driving through streets where children and their parents walk and play. Once we slow down, we may be surprised to notice God's care for the earth through the change of seasons and the return of migratory birds. When we slow down, we have time for our family, community and for God.

I invite each of you to take a small stone. Run your fingers over the stones, noticing its shape and texture. At the same time whisper a pray to God. See if you can hold the stone a little longer each day, increasing your time and attention on God. God enjoys our time in prayer. When we prayer we slow down.

Let us pray: Very patient God. Thank you for giving us time to come to you in prayer. Bless our children to learn to come to you and trust you and love you always. Amen

Lent 1

27 Promise Kept   Romans 4:1-5, 13-17

Supplies: Learn the old camp song "Father Abraham Has Many Sons." Make buttons with the slogan, "I am a Promise Kept"

A lesson for the heart

The moment you were born you were a promise kept. God promised the children born to Abraham's children would inherit the kingdom of God and God's righteous. God has kept that promise. There is an old bible camp song that will help you remember. Let's sing it together.

Chorus
Father Abraham has many sons
Many sons has father Abraham
I am one of the and so are you
So, let us praise the Lord!

Verse 1: Right Arm (raise right arm up and down).

Verse: 2: Left Arm (Raise both arms up and down).

Verse 3: Right Foot (Raise your right foot up and down).

Verse 4: Left Foot (Raise both feet alternatively)

You are a promise kept. Wear these buttons proudly telling the world who you are and whose you are.

Let us pray: God of Abraham and Sarah, thank you for keeping your promise and making us heirs to the kingdom. Bless these your children to continue the legacy and expand God's world. Amen

Lent 2

Supplies: A sample Nesting Doll set and small bags filled with paper clips, band-aids, paper hole reinforcers, plastic bread clips and rubber bands.

A lesson for the heart

The Slavic people are famous for dolls that nest inside one another. Each doll holds a doll, which holds a smaller doll. There can be as many as ten dolls nested in the first doll.

Like the nesting dolls, sometimes we think we have gotten through one problem only to find another problem waiting for us. It can be frustrating and make us very sad. God understands and pours love into our hearts to help us hold on and not give up.

In these bags are reminders of ways to hold on: a paper clip to keep things tidy, a rubber band for holding things in place, a band aid for the scrapes and cuts, paper hole reinforcers to repair the rips and a plastic bread tie to keep things fresh.

Let us pray: Almighty God, keep our children strong when things go wrong. Help them to hold on and trust you. Amen

Lent 3

Supplies: Neon light sticks

A lesson for the heart

The best way to remove the darkness is to turn on the light. Darkness cannot exist in the presence of light.

God has made you the light of the world. The best way to move the darkness is to turn on the light. Darkness cannot exist in the presence of light.

By turning on your light the darkness leaves. You are light when you are kind to the kids in your class.

You are light when help the neighbor with their groceries.

You are light when you give your parents a big hug when they come in from work.

Use these light sticks to move the darkness and to remind you to always be the light of world.

Let us pray: Holy God, thank you for making us the light of the world. Help our children to shine brightly every day. Amen

Lent 4

30 Palm-tastic!   Matthew 21:1-11

A lesson for the heart

When Jesus rode into Jerusalem on the small donkey the people lined the path with their clothes and palm branches.

They heard stories of Christ's love for others; the way Jesus healed the sick, made the blind to see and fed persons who were hungry. Jesus loved everyone well. But the greatest demonstration of the love of God would come a few days later—on the cross of Calvary. It is on the cross where God's love for humanity shines. God loves you so much that Jesus took all the bad of the world and turned that bad into love!

The palms are important and wonderful, but the cross is the real symbol of love.

I have taken a palm branch and folded it into a cross. As you go through this week hold on to your cross and try to love others the way God loves you---it may be hard, but it will bring its own reward.

Let us pray: Holy and gracious God, thank you for the cross. Thank you for loving us. Help our children to love themselves and others as you love them. Amen

Palm Sunday

31   Colored Eggs   John 20:1-8

Supplies: Colored eggs and enough Easter candy for the next two weeks.

A lesson for the heart

Colored eggs have been associated with death and rebirth for many thousands of years. Some of the first Christians only colored eggs red in memory of the blood of Christ from the cross.

For many the multi-colored eggs have become a symbol of the resurrection and are a large part of the festival we call Easter.

Whether your family purchased candy eggs or together you took time to dye your eggs, please think of Jesus' resurrection from the dead and the new life we have in Christ.

Christ is Risen.

Christ is Risen indeed!

Let us pray: Holy God, please bless these eggs and allow them to be good food. As we eat them help us to be thankful for the resurrection of Jesus Christ, who lives ad reigns with you and Holy Spirit forever. Amen

Resurrection Sunday

32 Thank You   Acts 2:1-14a

Supplies: Learn to say 'Thank you' in several languages. Choose from the list below and be sure to add languages common in your community. Easter candy.

A lesson for the heart

In English we say - Thank you

In Spanish we say – Gracias

In French we say – Merci (MEHR-see)

Japanese – (Domo) Arigato (ah-ree-GAH-toh)

Thai – Khop Khun (cap-coohn)

Luganda – Webale

Imagine a day when we would all understand God's promise in every language all at the same time. That day was the first Pentecost. God's spirit was poured out on all people and the word was salvation and life everlasting for all who believe in Jesus Christ.

The same is true today. Everyone who believes in Jesus Christ as Lord receives everlasting life.

We can say 'Thank you' to that and for more Easter Candy.

Let us pray: Loving God, pour your Spirit over our children and help the to hear your word of salvation and believe. Amen

Easter 2

33 Walk With Me   Acts 2: 14a, 22-32

Supplies: Candy Feet

A lesson for the heart

The chorus of an old church hymn goes something like this:

And God walks with me and God talks with me and God tells me I am God's own; and the joy we share as we tarry there, none other as ever known.[7]

After the resurrection, Jesus walked and talked with many people. Since Pentecost the promised Holy Spirit has been our constant companion, speaking God's peace into our hearts as we pray.

We can also hear Jesus speak to us as we read the bible. The bible is a living document and speaks of the power, peace and correction from God for every generation.

The good news: Jesus promises to walk with us and talk with us always.

Allow these 'feet' to encourage you to talk with Jesus in prayer and allow God to walk beside you your life long.

Let us pray: God, we are excited you keep your promises. Walk beside your children and speak to the along the way. Amen.

---

[7] "I Come to the Garden Alone" lyrics by Alan Jackson and Merle Haggard

Supplies: Bathroom size paper cups overflowing with goodies.

A lesson for the heart

A beloved psalm begins: "The Lord is my Shepherd, I lack nothing . . ."

It is said this hymn was written by Israel's great king, David. The hymn shows David's deep trust in God during the worst moments of David's life. David trusted God and shared with God's his fears and successes.

We can do the same. We can share our hopes, dreams and fears with our living and resurrected Saviour, Jesus Christ. When put our trust in God, we will live in green pastures and rest beside quiet waters. We will live in the house of the Lord our whole life long.

Like the life we live with God, these cups overflow with goodness. Enjoy

Let us pray: Generous God, thank you for pouring blessings over our children. Help them to trust you always. Amen

Easter 4

35   Don't Worry   John 14:1-14

Supplies: Learn Bobby McFerrin's song "Don't Worry, Be Happy"[8], Smiley face stickers.

A lesson for the heart

Parents worry. It is normal to worry. But not too much. A man named Bobby McFerin wrote a wonderful song about worry. When the adults in your life seem to be consumed with worry maybe a little of this song could help.

 (Sing one verse of the song) *Here's a little song I wrote, you 'wanna sing it note for note. Don't Worry, be happy. In every life, we have some trouble, but when you worry you make it double, don't worry, be happy.*

Let's sing together. (sing)

Sometimes singing can make us feel better. Remember this song and sing it loud and strong when the adults are tempted to worry too much.

After you sing the song give everyone a smiley face sticker as a reminder to cast their worries on God.

Let us pray: Gracious God, we don't want to worry too much. Help us to bring our worries and concerns to you in prayer and to sing, sing, sing. Amen

Easter 5

---

[8] Bobbie McFerrin, https://www.youtube.com/watch?v=d-diB65scQU
I DO NOT HAVE THE RIGHTS TO THIS SONG.

36   God Loves Me   John 14:15-21

Supplies: Bouquets of Colorful Flowers

A lesson or the heart

One way to know if the one you loved returned those affections is to use a flower. Take the flower by the stem and pull the petals off one by one. As you pull off the first petal say, They loves me.' When you pull off the second say, 'They loves me not.' Continue until all the petals are gone.

No matter how the flower test ends, you have this promise: God loves you. You were created in God's image and likeness. Jesus Christ died and rose from the dead so you may have life and have it to the fullest. God will never leave you alone. God's spirit has been sent to walk with you, guide you and encourage you as live and grow.

Take these flowers home, look at them and smile!

Let us pray: Thank you for Jesus; Christ's death and resurrection. Thank you for the promised Holy Spirit and the assurance of your love. Bless our children to feel and experience your love and to walk and grow in your peace. Amen

Easter 6

Supplies: Helium filled balloons on long strings

A lesson for the heart

Good things happen when we look up, we see the sun shining brightly, the beautiful birds overhead and if we are really paying attention a butterfly may come into view. Above our heads is wonder and beauty.

We cannot live life only looking up. We must also look around and live, work and share life with others.

God wants us to look up and get inspired by the beauty in our world and God wants us to look out and live the abundant life Jesus came and died to make possible.

I bet I can get you to look up! (release the strings and the balloons!)

Let us pray: Almighty God, thank you for the beauty of our world. Bless are children to see beauty and allow that beauty to inspire them to live well and share much. Amen

Ascension Sunday

Supplies: PRINT, H.E.L.P. in 72 font and lots of crayons.

A lesson for the heart

Jesus understood the need to pray. Scripture records many times when Saviour stopped and looked to God in prayer. Prayer is asking God for Help.

Dear Lord, **H**ear, my request,
> **Er**ase my worries, pain and fears
> **Le**t God be in control and give me
> **P**eace.

On these papers is the word HELP. Together we are going to add color in and around these letters. As you add the first color, think about what you want God to know; adding as little or as much as you want. With the second color ask God to erase any pain, worry or fears in your hearts. Add more color letting go of the problem and letting God take control and give you peace.

Prayer is sharing with God your inner most thoughts and trusting God is listening and will answer. Take these paper home and continue to add more color as you pray.

Let us pray together: Compassionate Saviour, thank you for hearing our inner most thoughts. Please help our children to ask you for help, daily and their life through. Amen

(Sybil Mac Beth is the author of *Praying in Color: Drawing a New Path to God* available through Paraclete Press. In her book Mac Beth details methods of using color and drawing to enhance and strengthen our prayer life. Her book is a great prayer resource.)

39   Honor Them   John 20:19-23

Supplies: Sweet and Sour Lollipops

A lesson for the heart

The story is told of a man who served in the military during World War II. The man's friends called him "Chappie". Chappie could be a bit difficult. Chappie drank more than socially. Chappie was not faithful to his spouse.

We would not call Chappie a 'good' man, with one exception: Chappie loved candy lollipops and didn't mind sharing with others.

These lollipops I share with you today are to remember Chappie's service during World War II and to honor all persons living and dead who served. We honor them not because they were 'good' but because they answered the call of God to serve. God sent them as God's sends us. We honor their sacrifice. We will always remember.

Let us pray: Merciful God, we thank you for the men and women who served and who serve in the armed services. Bless please their sacrifice and prosper their families according to your great riches in glory. On this Pentecost Sunday we pray the spirit of sacrifice be upon us all. Amen

Pentecost Sunday

40   Creation   Genesis 1:1-2,4a

Supplies: Twizzlers Pull and Peel Candy

A lesson for the heart

"In the beginning God created the heavens and the earth. Now the earth was formless and empty, darkness was over the surface of the deep and the spirit of God hovering over the waters. God saw that the light was good, and he separated the light from the darkness."

The creation story tells of God's care in creation, God's plan for redemption and God's companionship and guidance from Holy Spirit. All three working together to make the world we live in.

We talk about God as the Trinity, Father, Son and Holy Spirit, God is three in one and one in three.

It is not a perfect picture, but these Twizzlers candies are three in one and one in three. We can pull apart the candy and eat them separately and we can bite through all three at the same time. Three in one or one in three. God is good and sweet and wonderful, better than candy.

Let us pray: Holy God, thank you for creating the world we live in. Thank you for redeeming us through the blood of Jesus and thank you for your companionship through Holy Spirit. May our children know you in all the ways you are more each day. Amen

Trinity Sunday

41   Kazoo Noise   Psalm 100

Supplies: Kazoos

A lesson for the heart

I bet you can name a time someone thought you were making too much noise. You were playing and laughing and singing and then you heard, 'use your indoor voice' or 'play quietly'. Making noise can get us into a lot of trouble with our parents or teachers but not with God.

The psalmist (God's official poet) says, "make a joyful noise unto the Lord, all ye lands. Serve the LORD with gladness: come into his presence with singing."

The noise of worship and praise makes God smile.

When you are ready to make noise for God these kazoos will help. Blow songs of praise and thanksgiving to God. God who has been good and who is faithful to the young and the old will hear and smile.

Let us make some noise!!!

Let us pray: We praise you God with our songs and our noise. Bless our children to give thanks and praise you always. Amen

2nd Sunday June

Supplies: Chia Seed Kits[9] (chia seeds, dirt, small flowerpot, section of tights, googles eyes)

A lesson for the heart

Imagine counting the hairs on your head. Even if you could do it, it would take forever.

The good news: You don't need to God already has. God knows exactly the number of hairs on your head. God knows everything about you and is very pleased with everything about you—your size, eye color and even the number of hairs on your head.

You can get a tiny, tiny feeling of what it might be like to count the hairs on your own creation.

These kits contain what you need to grow 'hair' on a head of your making.

Let us pray: Thank you for knowing our children, loving them and watching over them as they grow. Bless them not to worry and to trust you always. Amen

3rd Sunday June

---

[9] Place a scoop of grass seed and then a scoop of dirt in the section of tights. Tie a knot and place the ball knot down into the small pot. Add the google eyes and draw a face with makers. Water the ball thoroughly and in 2-3 days the chia will sprout. Cut the 'hair' after around 10 days.

43   Buried   Romans 6:12-23

Supplies: M & M Peanut Candy

A lesson for the heart

To love and be loved by God is a little like being a peanut inside the M & M Candy[10].

First, like the deep chocolate coating, we are completely covered by sacrificial blood of Jesus.

Next, like the protective hard candy shell, the Holy Spirit protects and guides us; helping us move through life.

The good news: like the peanut buried in the center of the candy; when disappointment and sadness rains down, the protective shell does not melt for we are buried in the heart of Jesus Christ.

The best part: M & M are fun to eat!

Let us pray: We thank you God for burying our children deep in Christ Jesus. Please keep them there as they grow. Amen

4th Sunday June

---

[10] M & M Candy is a Mars Incorporated product. Please be careful of children with nut allegories.

44 Human Mistakes   Romans 7:15-25a

A lesson for the heart

Anytime we try something new like rollerblading or playing rugby or tennis there is a chance we will make a mistake. Yet, we need not hesitate or allow the fear of making mistake to keep us from trying.

Remember this – the only way to never make a mistake is to never do anything. Every man, woman, girl and boy we know has made a mistake or two; maybe three or four.

The good news is this: if the mistake hurts someone or something, God will forgive. No matter how many times, God is always ready to forgive us. God removes the stain of our mistakes and never sees them again.

These erasers are a reminder of God forgiveness. They are also handy for when you make your next mistake.

Let us pray: Gracious and merciful God, thank you for seeing our mistakes and loving us still. Forgive any mistakes our children have made and see those mistakes no more. Amen

1st Sunday July

45   Good Soil   Matthew 13:1-9, 18-23

Supplies: Small clear cups filled with cubes of chocolate cake,[11] a gummy worm, and topped with green sprinkles.

A lesson for the heart

Good soil has a few special attributes. Good soil is rich and sweet. Good soil attracts things like worms and other living cells. Things grow in good soil.

God has made you to be good soil. The soil of your hearts was made to be rich and sweet. We are made to attract others and we were made to share ourselves with them. When we are kind, generous and friendly are soil gets better and better.

This small cup is an example of good soil—chocolate cake! And in the 'soil' is a candy worm who was attracted to the rich sweet soil. To make it perfect it is covered in green sprinkles to represent the good things that grow on good soil. Eat the Cake. Be the good soil, growing sweeter each day!

Let us pray: God you are amazing! Thank you for making our children good soil. Bless them to grow sweeter and richer each day and to be a blessing to their families and to the world. Amen

2nd Sunday July

---

[11] DIY, bake a box chocolate cake in a 10 X15 X 1-inch jelly roll pan. Cut the cake into small squares and fill the cups.

Supplies: Buttons saying, 'God's Child'[12]

A lesson for the heart

Sometimes when a child is very young a special service is held, and the parents promise to share the ways of God with the child as she grows. Often two adults are asked to help the parents with this huge job. The adults are called, godparents. The child can count on the godparents to help.

On the day you were born God decided to help your parents with the huge task of making sure you grow up big and strong; you are God's child and along with your parents and earthly godparents you can always count on lean on and trust God to help.

Wear these buttons proudly, you are God's Child

Let us pray: Gracious God, our heavenly parent, thank you for your care, concern and help. Please help these children's parents and earthly godparents to give them all they need to grow, and stand chose by directly and encouraging, too. Amen

3rd Sunday July

---

[12] Creatology™ Plastic Buttons available at Michaels Stores

47   Bad Things Good People   Romans 8:26-39

Supplies: Blue ribbons

A lesson for the heart

Bad things do happen. Bad things happen to good people. Bad things happening is not a sign God does not care nor is it a sign God is absent.

God loves you and there is nothing you can do about it.

You are winning even when you are losing. God died so that you might have a great life.

You are #1 in God's kingdom.

People who are number one are awarded the blue ribbon. Wear this blue ribbon proudly showing the world your status in the kingdom.

You are number 1.

Let us pray: Thank you for thinking so much of us, you would die to make our lives better. Help the children to know how important they are to you, good times and bad. Amen

4th Sunday July

Supplies: Bubble Gum Tape to pass (I suggest one roll of tape for every ten children) and more for everyone to take home.

A lesson for the heart

Let us start with prayer. Dear God, we have X# rolls of bubble tape. We wish everyone to have some. Please bless this to be more than enough. Amen.

Please take a piece of gum and pass the roll to the next person.

A long time ago Jesus wanted to feed around 12, 000 men, women and children and started with 5 loaves of bread and 2 small fish. God prayed and there was more than enough. In God's kingdom there is always more than enough to share with others. Ask God to help you to be generous and kind. There are no shortages with God.

Take this roll of bubble tape and see how many people you can feed.

Let us pray: We thank you God you always have more than enough. Bless our children with abundance as they share all you will give them. Amen

1st Sunday August

49 Alphabet Soup   Matthew 14: 22-33

A lesson for the heart

One of the fun things about alphabet soup is making up words and then eating the words we find. With each spoonful we grow big and strong.

The bible is God's alphabet soup, the pages filled with words of comfort, peace, instruction and warning. When we 'eat' the word of God we grow into the people God would want—wise, understanding, compassionate and generous.

I recommend 'eating' some of the bible every day.

It may be a bit warm out for soup so, in these bags are alphabet cereal. Make some words, eat, grow and enjoy.

Let us pray: Thank you God for scripture, your alphabet soup. Help our children to take the words into their mouths and into their hearts and to one day share those words with others. Amen

2nd Sunday August

50   Good Food   Matthew 15:10-28

A lesson for the heart

When a person is on a diet it sometimes means managing the amount and type of food eaten. Some people count calories, measuring and weighing their food, so they don't eat too much. Some people eat only vegetables, they are called vegetarians. Others eat mostly meat and avoid processed foods and sweets; their diet is called Paleo.

Whichever diet you choose it is okay, God approves. God wants you eat and be healthy. No food is prohibited. God cares more about how we act, than what we eat.

God is kind and wants us to be kind.
God is love and God wants us to be loving.
God is forgiving, and God wants us to forgive.

I think God would even approve of these fine examples of candy fruit and vegetables. In small quantities, of course.

Let us pray: Generous God, you made the earth and everything on the earth. We thank you for good food. Help are children to make good diet choices and even better life choices. Amen

3rd Sunday August

Supplies: Bumblebee trading Card

A lesson for the heart

(singing) *I know I been changed. I know I been changed; I know I been changed; the angels in heaven done signed my name.*

The love of God shown in Jesus Christ changes us. We may not change on the outside like B-127[13] changes from an advanced bio-mechanical robot into a Volkswagen Beetle, named Bumblebee, but like love changed Bumblebee we do change on the inside

- Helping us make sacrifices for others
- Share our good fortune with those who have nothing
- Offer friendship when we have nothing to gain

This Bumblebee trading card is a visible reminder of the change possible when we are loved and when we love others as God loves us.

Let us pray: Merciful Saviour, bless our children with hearts open to love and with enough to share. Amen

4th Sunday August

---

[13] B-127 and **Bumblebee** are characters in a 2018 American science fiction action film centered on the *Transformers* character of the same name. It is the sixth installment of the live-action *Transformers* film series.

52   God's Call

Exodus 3:1-5

Supplies: Small notebooks

A lesson for the heart

Today when someone far away wants to talk with you, they use a mobile phone or connect through social media on the computer. But 1,200 years before Christ was born, the mobile phone had not been invented. God wanted to get Moses' attention and call Moses into service, so God used a burning bush.

God wants to call you into service in God's kingdom. I don't know what the service will be or when God will contact you, but I know how you will be ready, prayer.

When we speak to God regularly in prayer, God speaks to us in return. One way to pray is with a journal. Each day, write down what you want God to know, things you noticed, your hopes and dreams and even the sad parts of life. God hears and will answer and sometimes call.

Let us pray: Holy God, thank you for hearing us when we pray. Help our children to begin now speaking to you regularly so when you call, they will be ready to answer. Amen

5th Sunday August

About the Author

The Reverend Cheryle Renee-Chapman Hanna is the servant/leader at the Fourth Avenue Baptist Church in Ottawa, ON. The congregation boasts they are a FAB-ulous people, serving a fabulous God. Cheryle formerly served churches Toronto, Ontario, and Detroit, Michigan and is a requested preacher in both the U.S. and Canada.

Rev. Hanna was awarded a Doctor of Ministry degree from McCormick Theological Seminary in Chicago, Illinois; the thesis was in the practice of ministry: *Revitalizing Worship: Designing a Standard Order of Service for Fourth Avenue Baptist Church* and Rev. Hanna also received a Master of Divinity degree from Princeton Theological Seminary. Interestingly, she is also an engineer and holds a Bachelor of Mechanical Engineering degree from Kettering University which she put to good use in a former 14-year employment with General Motors. Located in Flint, Michigan, Kettering University is deeply tied to the development of the American automotive industry and was formerly known as the General Motors Institute.

Cheryle is married to Michael Curtis Hanna and they have raised four children; Natalie Randall (Kyler), Michael Anthony (Kel'Niesa), Adese, and William, and have four grandchildren, William Kato Hanna, II, Jackson Timothy Hanna, Simone Marie Randall, and Myles Pembroke Randall.

Matthew 17:1-9	Lesson 25	Transfigured
Matthew 21:1-11	Lesson 30	Palm-tastic!
Luke 14: 1, 7-14	Lesson 1	Table Talk
Luke 14: 25-33	Lesson 2	Brewster's Millions
Luke 15: 1-10	Lesson 3	Hide and Seek
Luke 16:1-3	Lesson 4	Choose Wisely
Luke 16:19-31	Lesson 5	Live Generously
Luke 17: 5-10	Lesson 6	Small Seeds
Luke 17:11-19	Lesson 7	Soapy Clean
Luke 18:1-8	Lesson 8	God is Fair
Luke 18:9-14	Lesson 9	Prayerful Hands
Luke 19:1-10	Lesson 10	Meeting Jesus
Luke 20:27-38	Lesson 11	Resurrection Cookies
Luke 21:5-10	Lesson 12	Jenga
Luke 23:33-43	Lesson 13	King Jesus
John 1: [1-0] 10-18	Lesson 19	Identity
John 14: 1-14	Lesson 35	Don't Worry
John 14:15-21	Lesson 36	God Loves Me
John 17: 1-11	Lesson 38	H.E. L.P.
John 20: 1-18	Lesson 31	Colored Eggs

Material for Additional Study

Armstrong, Thomas. *Multiple Intelligences in the Classroom*, Association for Supervision and Curriculum Development, 1999, ISBN: 0871202301.

Brown, Carolyn C. *You can Preach to the Kids Too! Designing Sermons for Adults and Children*. Abingdon Press, 1997. ISBN: 00687061571.

Bruce, Barbara. *7 Ways of Teaching the Bible to Children*. Abingdon, 1996. ISBN: 0687020689.

Gardner, Howard, *Frames of Mind: The Theory of Multiple Intelligences*. Basic Books, second anniversary. Edition, 1993. ISBN: 0465025102

Halverson, Delia. *Teaching Prayer in the Classroom: Experiences for Children and Youth*. Abingdon Press, 1989. ISBN: 0687064252

Knowles, Michael P., editor, *The Folly of Preaching: Models and Methods*, William B. Eermans Publishing Company, Grand Rapids, Michigan, 2007, ISBN: 978-0-8028-2465-3

McBeth, Sybil, *Praying in Color: Drawing a New Path to God*, Paraclete Press, Brewster, Massachusetts, 2009. ISBN 978-1-55727-512-9

Lickona, PH. D, Thomas. *Raising Good Children: Helping Your Child Through the Stages of Moral Development*. Bantum Books, 1994. ISBN: 055337429X

Tisdale, Leonora Tubbs, *Prophetic Preaching: A Pastoral Approach*, Westminster John Knox Press, 2010, ISBN: 978-0-664-23332-7

Osmer, Richard Robert. *Teaching for Faith: A Guide for Teachers of Adult Classes.* Westminster/John Knox Press, 1992. ISBN: 0664-252176

www.ingramcontent.com/pod-product-compliance
Lightning Source LLC
Chambersburg PA
CBHW031402060726

47590CB00007B/2906